Meet the KEY WORKERS

PEOPLE IN FOOD

BY
SHALINI VALLEPUR

BookLife PUBLISHING

©2022
BookLife Publishing Ltd.
King's Lynn
Norfolk PE30 4LS, UK

All rights reserved.
Printed in Poland.

A catalogue record for this book is available from the British Library.

ISBN: 978-1-80155-464-0

Written by:
Shalini Vallepur

Edited by:
John Wood

Designed by:
Jasmine Pointer

All facts, statistics, web addresses and URLs in this book were verified as valid and accurate at time of writing. No responsibility for any changes to external websites or references can be accepted by either the author or publisher.

Image Credits

All images are courtesy of Shutterstock.com, unless otherwise specified. With thanks to Getty Images, Thinkstock Photo and iStockphoto.

Cover – kurhan, Studio Romantic, melhijad, Vector_dream_team, Inspiring, Magnia, HappyPictures, Masa Marinkovic. 2–3 – Iakov Filimonov. 4–5 – VAKS-Stock Agency, vichie81. 6–7 – Olena Yakobchuk, Slatan, Budimir Jevtic, Inspiring. 8–9 – jongcreative, Tukaram.Karve, alicja neumiler, chung toan co, Radu Cadar. 10–11 – JP WALLET, HappyPictures, Monkey Business Images, Kwame Amo, Pogorelova Olga, maradaisy. 12–13 – Avigator Fortuner, Aleksandar Malivuk, Jarek Kilian. 14–15 – Inspiring, Dmitry Kalinovsky, SeventyFour, jc.space, 279photo Studio, Top Vector Studio, uiliaaa. 16–17 – robuart, gpointstudio, Kzenon, Iakov Filimonov. 18–19 – Pressmaster, Dmitry Kalinovsky, StockSmartStart, Pro Symbols. 20–21 – HASPhotos, Monkey Business Images, elenabsl, Gurza. 22–23 – Diego Cervo, CharacterFamily70.

CONTENTS

Page 4	Here to Help
Page 6	People in Food
Page 8	On the Farm
Page 12	On the Way
Page 14	In the Factory
Page 16	At the Supermarket
Page 20	Food Banks
Page 22	Food for Thought
Page 24	Glossary and Index

Words that look like **this** can be found in the glossary on page 24.

HERE TO HELP

There are lots of jobs in the world and each one is different. Some jobs are always needed. The people who do these jobs are called key workers.

Key can sometimes mean needed and important.

Firefighters are always needed in case there is a fire.

Firefighter

Without key workers, we would not have the things we need to live safely, such as food and important **services**.

PEOPLE IN FOOD

Have you ever been to a supermarket or food shop? Lots of food is sold in shops, but have you ever thought about how food is made?

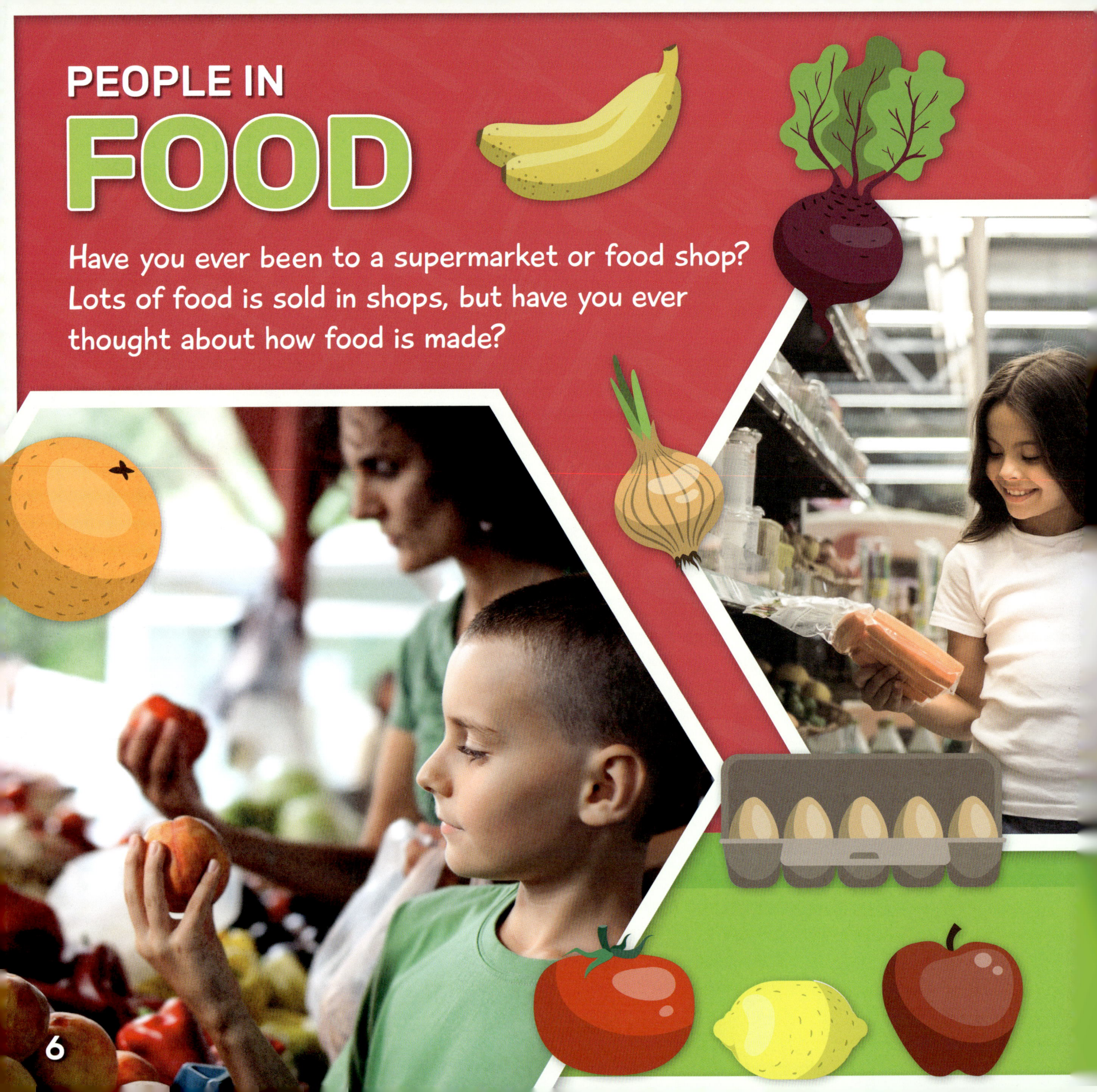

Who grows the food? And who makes sure that food gets to the shops? Lots of people work to make sure we have food. Let's learn all about them!

ON THE FARM

Most of the food that we buy starts off on farms. Farmers work hard all year round to grow **crops**. They plant the crops and care for them as they grow.

When the crops are ready for **harvest**, they are picked by farm workers and pickers. Crops may be picked by hand.

Working on a farm is tough!

Some farms use big machines, such as tractors, to harvest and carry crops. The farmers need special skills to use these machines.

Some farmers look after farm animals. If an animal is sick, the farmer may call a **vet**. Vets give **medicine** to sick animals and make sure they are well.

ON THE WAY

After being harvested, crops are usually taken to factories. Workers put the crops onto lorries or trains and they are taken to a factory.

Container ship

We get food from all over the world thanks to people working on container ships.

Sometimes crops are shipped around the world. Workers pack and put the crops onto aeroplanes or big container ships.

13

IN THE FACTORY

Crops are brought to factories where they are **processed** into lots of different food and packaged. Factory workers check the food and make sure that the factory machines are working properly.

Drivers use forklifts to carry food around the factory. When the food is ready to be sold, drivers load it onto lorries. Then, the lorries take the food to shops and supermarkets.

Crops can be turned into all sorts of food!

AT THE SUPERMARKET

Lots of people work in supermarkets and they are all here to help! Supermarket assistants put food onto the shelves when it arrives.

16

Bakers, butchers and fishmongers work at some supermarkets. They know all about the food that they serve and help us get the exact food we want.

When we are ready to pay for the food, we go to the cashier. The cashier adds up the cost of everything.

Supermarkets must be clean because there is a lot of food! Cleaners work hard to make sure everything is clean and tidy.

FOOD BANKS

A food bank is like a supermarket, but the food does not cost anything. Food banks get their food from **donations**.

Sometimes, people may not have enough to eat. A food bank can really help them.

Why not check if there are any food banks in your area that you can donate to?

Most food banks are run by volunteers. Being a volunteer means you do not get paid for the work you do. Volunteers work really hard to make sure people have enough to eat.

FOOD FOR THOUGHT

Lots of people work extremely hard to make sure we have food. Next time you eat something, think about where it came from and who helped to get it to the shops.

Always say thank you to the people who help!

Now you know about the people who work in food! Can you match each job below to the right person?

Farmer	Lorry driver	Supermarket assistant
Grows crops to eat	Drives crops to factories	Puts food on supermarket shelves

GLOSSARY

crops	plants that are grown on a farm
donations	things that have been given away for a cause such as a charity
harvest	when fully grown plants or crops are picked
medicine	something used or taken to fight off diseases
processed	changed or made into something else
services	tasks or actions that people pay other people to do, such as caring for older people, fixing things that are broken or cleaning
vet	a doctor who is trained to look after animals

INDEX

aeroplanes 13
animals 11
crops 8–10, 12–15, 23
factories 12, 14–15, 23
farms 8–11, 23

lorries 12, 15, 23
ships 13
supermarkets 6, 15–17, 19–20, 23
tractors 10

vets 11
volunteers 21